Published by BaoBao Bilingual Books

ISBN 978-1-998317-10-3

First Edition: November, 2023

Hello, Little Explorer!

Welcome to a world full of adorable animals! This book is specially made for sweet babies like you and your loving parents. Together, let's embark on a colorful adventure through the animal kingdom!

Your parents are here to share this journey with you, teaching you the names of these delightful creatures along the way.

So, get ready to giggle, point, and learn! Let's explore and have lots of fun together, discovering the names of these amazing animals.

Cat

猫 māo

I like to eat fish.

我喜欢吃鱼

wǒ xǐ huān chī yú

Dog
狗
gǒu

I like to eat bones.

我喜欢吃骨头

wǒ xǐ huān chī gǔ tou

Monkey

猴 hóu

I like to eat bananas.

我喜欢吃香蕉

wǒ xǐ huān chī xiāng jiāo

Mouse

鼠 shǔ

I like to eat cheese.

我喜欢吃奶酪

wǒ xǐ huān chī nǎi lào

Rabbit

兔 *tù*

I like to eat carrots.

我喜欢吃胡萝卜

wǒ xǐ huān chī hú luó bo

Chicken

鸡 jī

I like to eat worms.

我喜欢吃虫子

wǒ xǐ huān chī chóng zi

Tiger

虎 hǔ

I like to eat meat.

我喜欢吃肉

wǒ xǐ huān chī ròu

Fish

鱼 *yú*

I like to eat smaller fish.

我喜欢吃小鱼

wǒ xǐ huān chī xiǎo yú

Sheep

羊 yáng

I like to eat grass.

我喜欢吃草

wǒ xǐ huān chī cǎo

Cow

牛 niú

I like to eat grass, too.

我也喜欢吃草

wǒ yě xǐ huān chī cǎo

Horse

马 mǎ

I like to eat grass, too.

我也喜欢吃草

wǒ yě xǐ huān chī cǎo

Pig

猪 zhū

I like all foods.

我什么都喜欢吃

wǒ shén me dōu xǐ huān chī